Simplistic Beauty

Japanese Poetry

By P.S. Rowland

Dedicated to all who realize "Less is More"

© P.S. Rowland 2017

ISBN: 978-1-910115-80-0

This book is copyrighted under the Berne Convention
No reproduction without permission
All rights reserved.

Prepared for Publication by: LionheART Publishing House

The right of P.S. Rowland to be identified as the author of this work has been asserted by her in accordance with sections 77 and 78 of the Copyright, Designs and Patents Act 1988.

Other Books by P.S. Rowland

"Cut Both Ways"
Peaks and Valleys of a Passionate Relationship Expressed Through Poetry

This collection of works delves into the life of a relationship where both individuals are extremely artistic, intense, passionate about life, and fierce about love.

"Lest We Forget Life's Passion"

A collection of poetry that probes the intuitive language of the heart – the universal human experiences of love, nature, struggle and faith, through a combination of free verse poetry, rhyme and haiku.

Acknowledgments

A heartfelt thank you to my ever growing readership, and your continued love, support and appreciation for my craft. Love you all!

I'd like to express my gratitude to those close to me, who continue to encourage my writing career. You listen to me day in and day out, and allow me to use you as a sounding board. I appreciate your valuable input and feedback more than I could ever tell you. You're my heart and soul.

Table of Contents

Introduction i
Obscured – Haiku 1
Ball & Chain – Senryu 1
Personal Attachment – Senryu 2
Flutterbyes – Senryu 2
Instrumental Love – Senryu 3
Forever Love – Senryu 3
Love Covers All – Senryu 4
Love Nest – Senryu 4
Destined – Senryu 5
Shield – Haiku 5
Drab – Haiku 6
Love Material – Senryu 6
Snow Covers – Tanka 7
Fireflies – Haiku 7
Winter Growth – Haiku 8
Blues – Tanka 8
Love Time – Senryu 9
Heavy – Senryu 9
Seasons – Haiku 10
Havoc – Tanka 10
Dicey – Senryu 11
Hopeful – Haiku 11
Variance – Senryu 12
Feed – Senryu 12

Warmth – Haiku 13
Weatherglass – Haiku 13
Eternal – Senryu 14
Adverse – Tanka 14
Tranquility – Senryu 15
Runaway – Haiku 15
Plume – Haiku 16
Internal – Senryu 16
Changes – Tanka 17
Resilience – Haiku 17
Abyss – Senryu 18
Blighted – Tanka 18
Dead Dandy – Haiku 19
Unrest – Senryu 19
Elements – Tanka 20
Cracked – Senryu 20
Growth – Senryu 21
Escape – Haiku 21
Lancer of Love – Senryu 22
Seasons of Intimacy – Haiku 22
Enkindle – Senryu 23
"A" – Senryu 23
Memories – Haiku 24
I Choose You – Senryu 24
Sleepless – Senryu 25
Hush – Senryu 25
Neglect – Senryu 26
Splash – Haiku 26
Solid – Senryu 27

Rake – Haiku	27
Wild – Senryu	28
Foggy – Senryu	28
Baptize – Haiku	29
Insomnia – Tanka	29
Selfless – Senryu	30
Bleak – Senryu	30
Transfuse – Senryu	31
Scorch – Haiku	31
Springs Faith – Haiku	32
Matched – Senryu	32
Evolve – Haiku	33
Burning Bush – Tanka	33
Hidden – Senryu	34
Finally – Senryu	34
Inspiring – Haiku	35
Capture – Senryu	35
Phantom – Senryu	36
Nature's Band – Haiku	36
Clone – Senryu	37
Pretty Penny – Senryu	37
Float – Senryu	38
Urgency – Senryu	38
Wish Bone – Senryu	39
Mom – Senryu	39
Cluttering – Senryu	40
Limitless – Senryu	40
Sear – Senryu	41
Toeing the Line – Senryu	41

Vacant – Senryu 42
Playful – Senryu 42
Summer's Lust – Haiku 43
2016 – Haiku 43
Wither – Senryu 44
Blossoming – Senryu 44
Purr – Haiku 45
Solstice – Haiku 45
Love Farmer – Senryu 46
Worms – Haiku 46
Swirled – Senryu 47
Slipping – Haiku 47
No Air – Haiku 48
Cold – Haiku 48
Darkness – Senryu 49
Commence – Senryu 49
Rude – Senryu 50
Judgment – Haiku 50
Electricity – Senryu 51
Ringing – Haiku 51
Alone – Senryu 52
Autumn – Haiku 52
Encompass – Senryu 53
Falling – Haiku 53
My Private Sun – Senryu 54
Burning Pit – Senryu 54
London Fog – Haiku 55
Fall's Rainbow – Haiku 55
Cherished Solitude – Senryu 56

Diamonds – Haiku	56
Morning Sidewalk – Haiku	57
Evil Friends – Haiku	57
Insanity – Senryu	58
Saving Time – Haiku	58
Smothered – Senryu	59
Rooted – Senryu	59
Fall Rain – Haiku	60
Written in Stone – Senryu	60
My Light – Senryu	61
Morning Chill – Haiku	61
Soul Desire – Senryu	62
Misery – Senryu	62
Radiant – Haiku	63
Caress – Senryu	63
Last Breath – Senryu	64
Nature's Camera – Haiku	64
-18 Chill Factor – Haiku	65
Endurance – Senryu	65
Snowfall – Haiku	66
Picture Perfect – Haiku	66
Sunny Disposition – Haiku	67
Her Savior – Senryu	67
Gloom – Senryu	68
Lull- Haiku	68
Calvary – Senryu	69
Snow Blanket – Haiku	69
Cadence – Haiku	70
Placidity – Senryu	70

Pulsating Echo – Senryu 71
Succession – Senryu 71
Granddaughter – Senryu 72
Forage – Haiku 72
Sea of Flames – Haiku 73
Facade – Senryu 73
Inside – Outside – Haiku 74
Nights in White Cotton – Haiku 74
Evaporate – Haiku 75
Inconsistent – Senryu 75
Fallen – Senryu 76
Mercy – Senryu 76
Core – Senryu 77
Animalistic Contentment – Haiku 77
Boiling Point – Haiku 78
Zest – Senryu 78
Static Flow – Senryu 79
Cardinal – Haiku 79
Velvet – Haiku 80
Backfire – Senryu 80
Sol – Haiku 81
Chaos of Chatter – Haiku 81
End of Time – Haiku 82
Torment – Senryu 82
Luminosity – Haiku 83
Congestion – Senryu 83
Weak – Senryu 84
Blood Rose – Haiku 84
Our Story – Senryu 85

Invisible – Senryu	85
Widow – Senryu	86
Sage – Haiku	86
Spring Blows – Haiku	87
Captured – Senryu	87
Quail – Haiku	88
Lavender Diamonds – Haiku	88
Awaken – Senryu	89
Wind-Zero – Haiku	89
Borders – Haiku	90
Summer Storm – Haiku	90
Cleave – Senryu	91
Aging – Senryu	91
Divided – Senryu	92
Ravaged – Tanka	92
The Race – Senryu	93
Eventual – Senryu	93
Pain – Senryu	94
Kava – Senryu	94
Siamese – Senryu	95
Twin Flames	95
Inaction – Senryu	96
Waste of Time – Senryu	96
Burning Bush – Haiku	97
Absurdity – Senryu	97
Gravity – Senryu	98
Anima Gemella – Tanka	98
Bird Baths – Haiku	99
Haunt – Senryu	99

Tempest – Haiku 100
Typhoon – Haiku 100
Lavation – Senryu 101
Alyse Juree – Senryu 101
TT. – Senryu 102
M. – Senryu 102
Simplistic Beauty – Senryu 103
Tenacity – Senryu 103
First Snow – Haiku 104
Coddled – Haiku 104
Stand Strong – Senryu 105
The Hunt – Haiku 105

Introduction

Haiku is a non-rhyming form of poetry, consisting of 3 lines, in a 5-7-5 format of syllables. Its focus is on nature, and seasons. It involves the five senses, creating imagery and emotions, along with metaphors.

Senryu takes on the same form as Haiku; however the focus is on human nature and the ironies of life.

Tanka is a non-rhyming form of poetry, consisting of 5 lines, in a 5-7-5-7-7 format of syllables, giving a complete picture of a mood or event.

Simplistic Beauty

Japanese Poetry

Simplistic Beauty

Obscured – Haiku

Heaven all around
Chatter drifting in and out
Unsettling dank fog.

Ball & Chain – Senryu

Marriage is a word
Not many investigate,
Ties that bind all time.

P.S. Rowland

Personal Attachment – Senryu

Warmth and love between
Urges met, some left unseen
Sink deep inside me.

Flutterbyes – Senryu

Butterfly touches
Gently stroking of my heart
Stab my heart with yours.

Simplistic Beauty

Instrumental Love – Senryu

Ring my bells softly,
Strum my inner core sweetly
Your passion saves me.

Forever Love – Senryu

The depth of your heat
Singes my skin as you touch
Branding me as yours

P.S. Rowland

Love Covers All – Senryu

Stiffness surrounds me
Cold, and trembling in my soul
Cover me with love.

Love Nest – Senryu

Filaments cloak us
Heat radiating inside
Passion, combustion.

Destined – Senryu

Together we stand
Uninvited yet fated,
Soulmates forever.

Shield – Haiku

Glistening pupils
Shield and protect, snow blindness,
Frozen sun blazing.

Drab - Haiku

Brown, white, brown, white, brown
Depressing, dark, ugliness
Winter days forlorn.

Love Material - Senryu

Silky as satin
Trembling under your sweet touch
Passion inside me.

Snow Covers – Tanka

Winter piléd in
Covering over my sin,
Forgiveness in cold
Springing forth to the pure light,
Walking forward in my plight.

Fireflies – Haiku

Lightning rain falls down
Blue oceans above our heads,
Wings with glowing tails.

Winter Growth - Haiku

Sprigs spring forth from white,
Rising towards yellow heat,
Devastating cold.

Blues - Tanka

Soaking heavy gray
Breathe deeply through the thickness,
Winter depression
Seeping from your inner bone
Bring life to me with sunshine.

Love Time – Senryu

Beating through to love
Ticking deep within my chest,
The hour has arrived.

Heavy – Senryu

Pressure to conform,
I will never be enough
My spirit is crushed.

Seasons – Haiku

Air patterns shifting,
Cold drifting away from me,
The sun has kissed me.

Havoc – Tanka

Light blazing throughout
Caressing my soft, tanned legs
Bitten by cold wind.
Elements can love and hate
Bare our souls to nature's gate

Dicey – Senryu

Sentiment of love,
Erratic thoughts in our mind
Biased and vacant.

Hopeful – Haiku

Brown throughout my eyes,
Warm yellow stroking my skin
The day will brighten.

Variance – Senryu

Taunting my love source,
Black and white contrasting views
Evil and goodness.

Feed – Senryu

Comfort in silence
Centering my heart and mind,
Self-nurturing now.

Warmth – Haiku

Beg, let me inside
Meowing at his loudest
Here, kitty kitty.

Weatherglass – Haiku

Low, dense, silver sky
Lethargy heavy inside,
Storm gauge is acute.

Eternal - Senryu

How deep can he go,
Within the process of her?
To the bitter end.

Adverse - Tanka

Natural ground glass
Rippling from each side to side,
Pretty face askew
Dampness flowing inside me,
Bitterness flowing over.

Tranquility – Senryu

Dip deeply inside,
The warmth, softness surrounds you,
Pull the plug on me.

Runaway – Haiku

Shimmering, glassy
Droplets accelerate down,
Preserved by the pane

Plume – Haiku

Chilled, dark morning air
Forced out by blazing fire,
Smoke signals of love.

Internal – Senryu

Inadequacy
Imperfect, blemished and weak,
Your distorted view.

Changes - Tanka

Subtle hints of spring
Standing on the edge of now,
Straining to hear you,
The cold is driving away,
The warmth ignites our beings.

Resilience - Haiku

Yellow, bright and warm,
Snow shrinking back its edges,
Tropical I'd be.

Abyss – Senryu

Pain, cracks, deep within
Fastened inside this crevasse,
I long to break free.

Blighted – Tanka

Dark, porous and cold,
Activity has left me,
Black is my color.
Support my downheartedness,
My triumph will be my own.

Dead Dandy - Haiku

Sticks with cones on top,
Cotton fibers caught by wind,
Flower is extinct.

Unrest - Senryu

The war within him
Churning his emotions black,
Stop playing the game.

Elements - Tanka

Crunch beneath my feet
Drudgery with every step,
Tangled brush sky high.
Wind and dust are irritants
Ripples of water will cleanse.

Cracked - Senryu

The daggers she throws
Embedded deep inside him,
Breaking her own heart.

Growth – Senryu

For the love of all
Within your beautiful heart,
Step inside your mind.

Escape – Haiku

Peeking through the brown,
Driven to expose itself,
Blossoming beauty.

Lancer of Love – Senryu

Give the edge of you,
Pierce my shell and let me live
Piece me together.

Seasons of Intimacy – Haiku

Bright, blinding and warm
Peeling layers as we go,
Spring has sprung, let's live.

Enkindle - Senryu

When left in darkness
The heart will shrivel and die,
Revive with a kiss.

"A" - Senryu

Beautiful at birth,
Angelic as she transformed,
Love my precious girl.

Memories – Haiku

Flickers, orange, red
Lapping heat against my skin,
Stories, cocoa, love.

I Choose You – Senryu

Choices we must make
Stability or passion,
The love of my life.

Simplistic Beauty

Sleepless – Senryu

Deep in the shadows
Tossing until morning light,
The walking dead rise.

Hush – Senryu

Dip into my eyes
Our deep blue waters of love,
Dry my tears for you.

Neglect – Senryu

The lack of all words,
No feeling conveyed at all
Has left me lonely.

Splash – Haiku

Ripples like satin
Evaporating above,
Stomped by all children.

Simplistic Beauty

Solid – Senryu

Touch her inner core
Please her from all directions,
You are her life mate.

Rake – Haiku

Cleaning with tongue braille
Choking on hair deep inside,
Cat cleaning is crude

P.S. Rowland

Wild – Senryu

Chills and anxiousness
Excitement and nervousness,
He owns my body.

Foggy – Senryu

Exhaustion rips me
Indecision is deadly,
My life is not mine.

Baptize - Haiku

Glisten in the rays,
Wet rainbows spread across lawn,
Worms dance in gladness.

Insomnia - Tanka

Solitude abounds.
Padded cotton around me
Lost in fogginess,
No thoughts connect together
Standing on the edge, empty.

Selfless – Senryu

She's weak and fragile
Requiring strength from his heart
Stand up, be the man.

Bleak – Senryu

Stricken in my soul
You are who I want right now,
Lost and desolate.

Transfuse – Senryu

He feeds me life's food
Love penetrating within,
  Forever my man.

Scorch – Haiku

Hot, humid, dripping
Pungent smells rising between,
  Summers burning fire.

Springs Faith - Haiku

Flowery fragrance
Pink and delicate abounds,
Dogwoods do not bark.

Matched - Senryu

Please have faith in me
Trust my beating heart in yours,
We are of like kind.

Evolve – Haiku

Emerging color
Popping forward so boldly,
Spring to the present.

Burning Bush – Tanka

Red spreads to the end
Splayed like a Japanese fan
Shielding those around,
Rooted deep into the earth
Fire erupting through eyes.

Hidden – Senryu

Pain deep inside us
Begging to be released soon,
Ugliness abounds.

Finally – Senryu

Golden gates of love
Opened, releasing pure joy
Flowing between us.

Inspiring - Haiku

Creeping vine so tall,
Cresting through each bloom it bears,
Creation explained.

Capture - Senryu

Hot and sensual,
His voice triggers my heart's love
Shot down by Cupid.

Phantom – Senryu

Unattainable,
Grasping at straws out of reach,
Contentment eludes.

Nature's Band – Haiku

Music, soothing sounds
A symphony amongst wild,
The feathered tweeters.

Clone – Senryu

Closing film on eyes,
You fail to see her errors,
Perfection you need

Pretty Penny – Senryu

Bling, glitter and love
Claim your one with diamond rings,
Marriage is costly.

Float – Senryu

Rush and panic me,
Let me breathe slowly myself
Gliding breezily.

Urgency – Senryu

The love of my life
Is just out of reach to me,
Come into my heart

Wish Bone – Senryu

The crossroads is here.
Time to make a decision.
Is it life or death?

Mom – Senryu

Her comforting arms
Her calming voice to my heart,
Miss my mom so much.

P.S. Rowland

Cluttering – Senryu

Sorrowing and ache
Love, joy, contentment and you,
How do I fix it?

Limitless – Senryu

Come hither, please touch,
My heart is yours forever
The future is ours

Sear – Senryu

Tender tips of lips
Explore the sensual heat,
Desires exploding.

Toeing the Line – Senryu

With sun in my eyes
I ponder through my hot tears,
Is this all there is?

Vacant – Senryu

Bare my soul to you,
Silence is what you return.
A slow death of us.

Playful – Senryu

Loving you is fun,
Energized by your presence
You seal the love deal.

Summer's Lust - Haiku

Satiating sun
Boiling in my love for you
Kissed by the fire

2016 - Haiku

Fireworks do kiss
Three hundred, sixty five days,
The new year begins.

Wither – Senryu

What is love to you?
Do you know what is needed?
My soul is dying.

Blossoming – Senryu

What is love to you?
Communication and trust.
My soul is thriving.

Purr - Haiku

Golden marble eyes
Jet black, velvet cloak surround,
Feline perfection.

Solstice - Haiku

Sweltering behind
Droplets descending downward,
The sun is crying.

Love Farmer – Senryu

He digs in my mind,
Cultivating emotions
Plowing my heart fields.

Worms – Haiku

Tweets and squeaks abound,
Chaotic and rushed to eat,
Playing tug of war.

Swirled – Senryu

Confusion and love,
Pain and happiness fill me,
Settled I am not.

Slipping – Haiku

Warmth is spiraling,
Days recede into the night,
Autumn is winning.

No Air - Haiku

Breathing gray flannel,
Wet eyes as we peer through it.
Smoke from fires choke.

Cold - Haiku

Gray, dark and angry
Drizzling, wet, damp, and ugly,
Hibernate with me.

Darkness – Senryu

When the night surrounds,
Alone I do find myself
Lost in thoughts of you.

Commence – Senryu

Laughter, tears and joy
Giggles, fun and excitement,
Blending of the hearts.

Rude – Senryu

Manners, kindness and
Graciousness are a lost art,
Selfishness presides.

Judgment – Haiku

Eyes peering through fog
Damp within my aching heart,
Do I love and die?

Simplistic Beauty

Electricity – Senryu

Piercing looks between,
Connected on deep levels
Burning desirés.

Ringing – Haiku

Listen in silence
Chaos breaks out in your ears,
Tone deaf yet alive.

Alone – Senryu

She desperately needs,
He's incapable to give,
Hollow in the cold.

Autumn – Haiku

Orange, yellow, brown
Trickling down from the blue sky,
Perfect maple leaves.

Encompass – Senryu

Tenderly he loves,
Savage lion protecting,
The perfect lover.

Falling – Haiku

All is slowing down.
Frost covers the surfaces,
Gloom is impending.

My Private Sun – Senryu

Life around me is
Slow motion, stagnant, hollow
Until your face shines.

Burning Pit – Senryu

Drained of every strength,
Searing emotions burn me,
Curled up and aching.

London Fog - Haiku

Milky air floating
Damp against my skin so deep,
Misting heavily.

Fall's Rainbow - Haiku

Green, orange, red, brown
Fiery, beauty displayed,
Melting to the ground.

Cherished Solitude – Senryu

Coffee, pen and pad
Words and musical notes float,
Fireworks burst forth.

Diamonds – Haiku

Ceiling of starlight
Glittering shadows on me,
Twilight in secret.

Morning Sidewalk – Haiku

Ground splattered in gold,
Crispy maple leaves to kick
Crunch beneath my feet.

Evil Friends – Haiku

Frosted peaks covered,
Round globes perched upon the stairs,
Gargoyle, dark faces.

Insanity – Senryu

Calmness and quiet,
Her mind and heart are begging
Never to receive.

Saving Time – Haiku

Early, yet is dark
Changing of time means nothing,
Waking black, sleep black.

Simplistic Beauty

Smothered – Senryu

He rises for her,
Each thought and movement for her,
She can't breathe for him.

Rooted – Senryu

All around the world,
I only see you and me
Our minds, hearts, and souls.

Fall Rain - Haiku

A tear rolling down,
Etched windows obscuring love
God cried down for us.

Written in Stone - Senryu

Rapture in his eyes,
Love, devotion, cemented
Radiating love.

My Light – Senryu

He brightens my core
Lifts my spirit when I'm down,
Saves my lonely heart.

Morning Chill – Haiku

Drifting slowly by,
Caught in the current of fall,
Cutting to my core.

Soul Desire – Senryu

Sparkle in his eyes,
Glint of passion, teasing, love,
Infinity-mate.

Misery – Senryu

Pressure in my face,
Pain slicing through my dead smile,
Medicate me numb.

Simplistic Beauty

Radiant – Haiku

Twisted vines of wood,
Backdrop for iced rays of sun,
Brilliant, sunny day.

Caress – Senryu

Gently touch my bones,
Fragile, and tender as me.
My strength forever.

P.S. Rowland

Last Breath – Senryu

Smell my inner self
Inhale my beauty, exhale.
Lay with me till death.

Nature's Camera – Haiku

Shadows across leaves
Drawn in beautiful designs,
Casting a soft light.

-18 Chill Factor – Haiku

Gale winds slice through her,
Chatter wracks her aching bones,
Blizzardly insane.

Endurance – Senryu

Happy and sadness
Mixed within his heart and soul,
Striving for his goal.

Snowfall - Haiku

Wet, crystal velvet
Floating beautifully down,
Piléd high for all.

Picture Perfect - Haiku

I like the winter
scene, when tucked inside warmly,
Drinking hot cocoa.

Sunny Disposition – Haiku

Emanating heat
To dispel the bitter cold,
Blasting out winter

Her Savior – Senryu

Loneliness set in,
Subtle rejection she feels,
He revives her will.

Gloom – Senryu

Dejected outside,
Afraid for feelings inside,
Her eyes see sadness.

Lull - Haiku

Breathe the milky air.
Stagnant, thick, heavy in lungs,
Winter seduction.

Simplistic Beauty

Calvary – Senryu

Help is on the way,
To soothe your aching sorrows
Kneel and pray with me.

Snow Blanket – Haiku

Brown covered in white,
Quiet, sleepy, no movement.
Snow covers all sin.

Cadence – Haiku

Drip it down, up, up.
Symphony of the droplets
Splashing to the beat.

Placidity – Senryu

Climb on into me
My heart and soul are waiting,
Soothe my aching parts.

Pulsating Echo - Senryu

Resonating love
Pounding loud and clear for her,
She flows through my veins

Succession - Senryu

Bone-cold and shaky,
Life slipping by at high speed
And then the end comes.

Granddaughter – Senryu

Laughter in her eyes,
Smiles that melt my inner self,
Tiny hand in mine.

Forage – Haiku

Hunger within him,
Hooves scrape the ground while searching
Nature's empty plate.

Simplistic Beauty

Sea of Flames – Haiku

In the darkened morn,
Flames flicker to warm the air
Conquering the cold.

Facade – Senryu

Whispered I LOVE YOU,
Then abandoned me behind
Lonely in the drought

P.S. Rowland

Inside – Outside – Haiku

Speckled dark and light,
Temperatures are hot and cold,
Burning bush and snow.

Nights in White Cotton – Haiku

Fog drifting along
Stifling my view of distance
Spring is pushing through.

Simplistic Beauty

Evaporate – Haiku

First green peeking through,
White ice retreating slowly,
Disappearing act.

Inconsistent – Senryu

He loves and hates me.
Words say love, actions say hate,
I need both, please leave.

Fallen – Senryu

The darkness seeps in,
Covering her light inside.
Emotions are flat.

Mercy – Senryu

Taste my ruby lips,
Suck nectar from my body,
Consume every inch.

Simplistic Beauty

Core – Senryu

Laughter, joy, and love
Smiles, compassion, contentment,
Family is everything.

Animalistic Contentment – Haiku

Rolled into a ball
Like a fuzzy skein of yarn,
Purring and licking.

P.S. Rowland

Boiling Point - Haiku

Blinding rays of sun
Heating up my bone marrow,
Heatwave acknowledged.

Zest - Senryu

Life flows though my blood
When I am with him, and when
He leaves, I am dead.

Static Flow – Senryu

Happy with nothing,
Contentment is elusive,
Constantly needing.

Cardinal – Haiku

Whistled songs in flight,
The tale of crisp beginnings,
The first day of spring.

Velvet - Haiku

Nectar in a cup,
Invigorating substance,
Java love affair.

Backfire - Senryu

His heart burst open.
A million pieces of life
Scattered to the ground.

Sol - Haiku

Heat upon my bones
Revitalizing my soul.
I'm sun worshipping.

Chaos of Chatter - Haiku

Feathers, wings, and beaks
Tweeting, at such lightning speeds,
In-flight happiness.

End of Time - Haiku

Hands straight and narrow
Ticking as time pushes forth,
Tick tock, tick tock, stop.

Torment - Senryu

I dream, silent death.
Awakened to the panic,
Heart bursting with fear.

Simplistic Beauty

Luminosity - Haiku

Sun setting so low,
Fire touching land and sea
Warming our insides.

Congestion - Senryu

I have a burning
Desire to drown the wicked
From suffocation.

Weak - Senryu

Love, guts and glory.
She craved love and guts from him,
His glory he chose.

Blood Rose - Haiku

Fragrant, velvet soft
Deep red, yellow, white and pink
Bleeding from the thorns.

Our Story – Senryu

Cover to cover,
I want to get lost with you
In pages of life.

Invisible – Senryu

Disconnected thoughts,
Clouds float around my being
Spitting butterflies.

Widow - Senryu

Disturbed and shattered,
Her aura is dark and cold,
Tangles in her web.

Sage - Haiku

Lavender spears shine,
Emit perfume in the air
Swaying in sweet dance

Simplistic Beauty

Spring Blows – Haiku

Whistling past our ears,
Twirling hair like a blender,
Aggravating wind.

Captured – Senryu

Rapidly sinking
Into the softest of hearts,
Death grip on my soul.

Quail - Haiku

Cluckers chattering,
Fending off the predators.
Beauty in the crown.

Lavender Diamonds - Haiku

Misty lavender.
Crystal droplets gently touch
Spikes of purple, reign.

Awaken – Senryu

The heat of the sun
Warmed her coffee laden soul,
A.M. ecstasy.

Wind-Zero – Haiku

As still as cement,
Stagnant against all forces,
No air to breathe in.

Borders- Haiku

Peeking purple eyes,
Beautiful and standing tall,
Glory in God's gifts.

Summer Storm - Haiku

Silence in raindrops,
Patterns of light reflecting,
Gray clouds exploding.

Cleave – Senryu

Around his body
I cling for his love of me,
Threaded forever.

Aging – Senryu

Creaking of my bones
Reflecting over my years,
Hindsight helps no one.

Divided – Senryu

Battered in my heart,
There is no peace surrounding.
Help me break away.

Ravaged – Tanka

The sting of the heat
Creates holes into my heart.
Then cooled with kisses,
Pulling myself together,
I lay my mind down to rest.

Simplistic Beauty

The Race – Senryu

Sweat from my brow drips,
Pounding feet bring me closer
To my goals of life.

Eventual – Senryu

The hero she knew,
Encased in her wanting heart
Came into her reach.

Pain – Senryu

The pain is so deep
I seek to make my way out,
Failed at the attempt.

Kava – Senryu

Heaviness surrounds
The beat of her sleepy heart,
Awakened by Joe.

Simplistic Beauty

Siamese – Senryu

Side by side they sit,
Anxiously awaiting love.
Life depends on it.

Twin Flames

Within the pages of my heart
Beats the love of a lifetime,
It's YOU, it's ME, it's US.

Inaction - Senryu

I hear your heartbeat,
The sound is faint over time,
I've already left.

Waste of Time - Senryu

The lies you put forth
Are more effort than the truth.
I believe nothing!

Burning Bush - Haiku

Floating, yet tethered,
Tinsel reflects on each one,
Wet leaves on the vine.

Absurdity - Senryu

Games we play out loud,
Dreams we hold inside our hearts,
Straining to live it.

Gravity – Senryu

Impending bad news
Deeply shook the core of me,
Doctors are not friends.

Anima Gemella – Tanka

The love of my heart
Is the strongest beat I've known.
He's fully present,
Leaves nothing to interpret,
Satisfies my very soul.

Bird Baths - Haiku

Dodging back and forth,
Playing peekaboo with you,
Wet from the sprinkler.

Haunt - Senryu

Pain around my ribs
Controlling my every move,
Heal my broken heart.

Tempest – Haiku

He opens his eyes,
Wetness surrounds every breath,
Hurricane drenching.

Typhoon – Haiku

Crimson shades of lace
Dancing to her ghost lover.
Gusts at eighty-five.

Lavation – Senryu

Clearing out cobwebs
From the corners of her heart
With leaded scalpels.

Alyse Juree – Senryu

Deep inside of me,
She moves in all her wisdom.
Her lessons live on.

TT. – Senryu

Her sweet smile lifts me.
I like pie and butterflies
Crested in my heart.

M. – Senryu

Bouncing off the walls,
She's giggles and energy
Gifting life to all.

Simplistic Beauty - Senryu

Deep breath, slowly in,
Reflect inside your body.
Exhale the toxic.

Tenacity - Senryu

Determined lover
Running top speeds for my heart,
Action always wins.

P.S. Rowland

First Snow - Haiku

Cotton drifting down.
Dizziness, with the swirling
White, covering sin.

Coddled - Haiku

Tucked in and away,
Branches surrounding feathers,
Eating seeds with love.

Simplistic Beauty

Stand Strong - Senryu

Strength comes from within.
Immune to his craziness,
Let him die alone.

The Hunt - Haiku

Crisp, white, shadows hang.
Coyotes run, hunt for food,
My cats want in now.

www.ingramcontent.com/pod-product-compliance
Lightning Source LLC
LaVergne TN
LVHW041546070426
835507LV00011B/954